First Facts

Primary Source Pro

Research Primary Source Artifacts

Tools, Clothing, Coins, and More!

by Kelly Boswell

PEBBLE
a capstone imprint

First Facts are published by Pebble
1710 Roe Crest Drive, North Mankato, Minnesota 56003
www.mycapstone.com

Library of Congress Cataloging-in-Publication Data
Library of Congress Cataloging-in-Publication-Data is on file with the Library of Congress.
ISBN 978-1-9771-0290-4 (library binding)
ISBN 978-1-9771-0514-1 (paperback)
ISBN 978-1-9771-0294-2 (ebook pdf)

Editorial Credits
Erika L. Shores, editor; Charmaine Whitman, designer; Jo Miller, media researcher; Laura Manthe, production specialist

Image Credits
Alamy: Art of Advertising, 11, B Christopher, 21; Getty Images: Ariel Skelley, 5, Santi Visalli/Contributor, 15; Shutterstock: Adrio Communications Ltd, 17, bigjom jom, Cover (bottom left), Leon Rafael, 9, Mark_Kostich, 7, nito, Cover (top left), s74, 13, Sibrikov Valery, Cover, (top right), Yellow Cat, Cover (bottom right); Wikimedia: Pratt & Letchworth, 18–19

Design Elements
Shutterstock: Nucleartist

Printed and bound in the United States of America.
1869

Table of Contents

What Is a Primary Source Artifact?

Have you ever been to a yard sale? The items for sale can tell you about the people who are selling them. You might be able to tell if the family has kids or if they like to cook. These items are examples of **primary source artifacts**. Artifacts help us learn about the past.

primary source—an original, first-hand account of an event or time period

artifact—an object that has been made or shaped by humans

Different Kinds of Primary Source Artifacts

Tools, household items, clothes, and coins are kinds of primary source artifacts. Artifacts are objects made or shaped by people. We can see them and touch them. Artifacts give us clues about everyday life in the past or about important people in history.

Fact

Ben Franklin was never a U.S. president. But he was important in U.S. history. He helped write the **Declaration of Independence**. He also helped create the first library in the United States.

Declaration of Independence—a document signed on July 4, 1776, declaring the United States' independence from British rule

We know when a coin was created because the date is on it. We can tell that Ben Franklin was an important person because his face is on a U.S. coin.

Tools are another kind of primary source artifact. When you **examine** artifacts like these, look carefully. Think about the people who made and used this tool. What can we learn about them by looking at the tool?

Fact

The mano and metate were made by the Sinagua people sometime between 1100 and 1400. The Sinagua people lived in what is now Arizona.

examine—to inspect or look at something carefully

The mano part was made using a rounded stone.
Metates were made using a flat, rough stone.
Corn kernels were placed on the metate. Then the mano was rubbed back and forth over the kernels until they became flour.

This camera is another kind of artifact. It doesn't look like the cameras we use now. Today, cameras are smaller and easier to use. Many people take photographs using the camera that is built right into their phones!

Fact

The world's first photograph was taken in 1826 by Joseph Nicéphor Niépce. He took a picture from his upstairs window in France.

To use the camera, a person needed to put film in it.

The film could later be developed into pictures.

This camera was made in the 1930s.

Looking, Learning, Wondering

When you look at artifacts like this typewriter, imagine using a magnifying glass to notice every detail. Start at one end and look carefully at everything!

Think about these questions:

- When you first look at the artifact, what comes to mind?
- What are you wondering?
- In what ways is this typewriter similar to a computer?
- How is it different?

This typewriter was sold in the late 1800s and early 1900s. A piece of paper was placed into the top and you typed on the paper. Today, we type on computers.

Clothing is another kind of primary source artifact.

One way to study and write about artifacts is to answer the "Five W Questions:"

Who?	Who made the artifact? Who used it?
What?	What is it used for? What is it made from?
Where?	Where was the artifact used?
When?	When was it used?
Why?	Why do you think it was made?

What: Look closely at the shirt. It is made from animal hides, horsehair, and wool.

Who: We can't tell who made this shirt. The shirt was worn by men in the Nez Percé tribe.

Where: The shirt comes from the Nez Percé tribe. We can assume it was worn where the tribe lived—in the northwest part of the United States.

When: We can't know for sure, but **historians** believe this shirt was made in 1850.

Why: Perhaps this shirt kept the person warm on cold days. Or maybe the shirt was worn only for special occasions or dancing.

historian—a person who studies history and writes about it

Your turn! Use the "Five W Questions" to study this old telephone.

Who?	Who might have made the artifact? Who might have used it?
What?	What is it used for? What do you think it might be made from?
Where?	Where was this made?
When?	When were phones like this used?
Why?	Why do you think this was made?

Using Other Sources

Often you won't be able to answer all of the questions just by looking at the artifact. You will need to use books, websites, and other sources.

Digging Deeper

This toy was made in the early 1900s. Kids played with it the way kids today play with toy fire trucks. If we held this toy, we might be able to tell how it works and what it's made out of. We wouldn't know how much it cost or if it was a common toy at that time.

Looking at a toy like this, we can see how much fire-fighting equipment has changed. The fire engines we see today look very different.

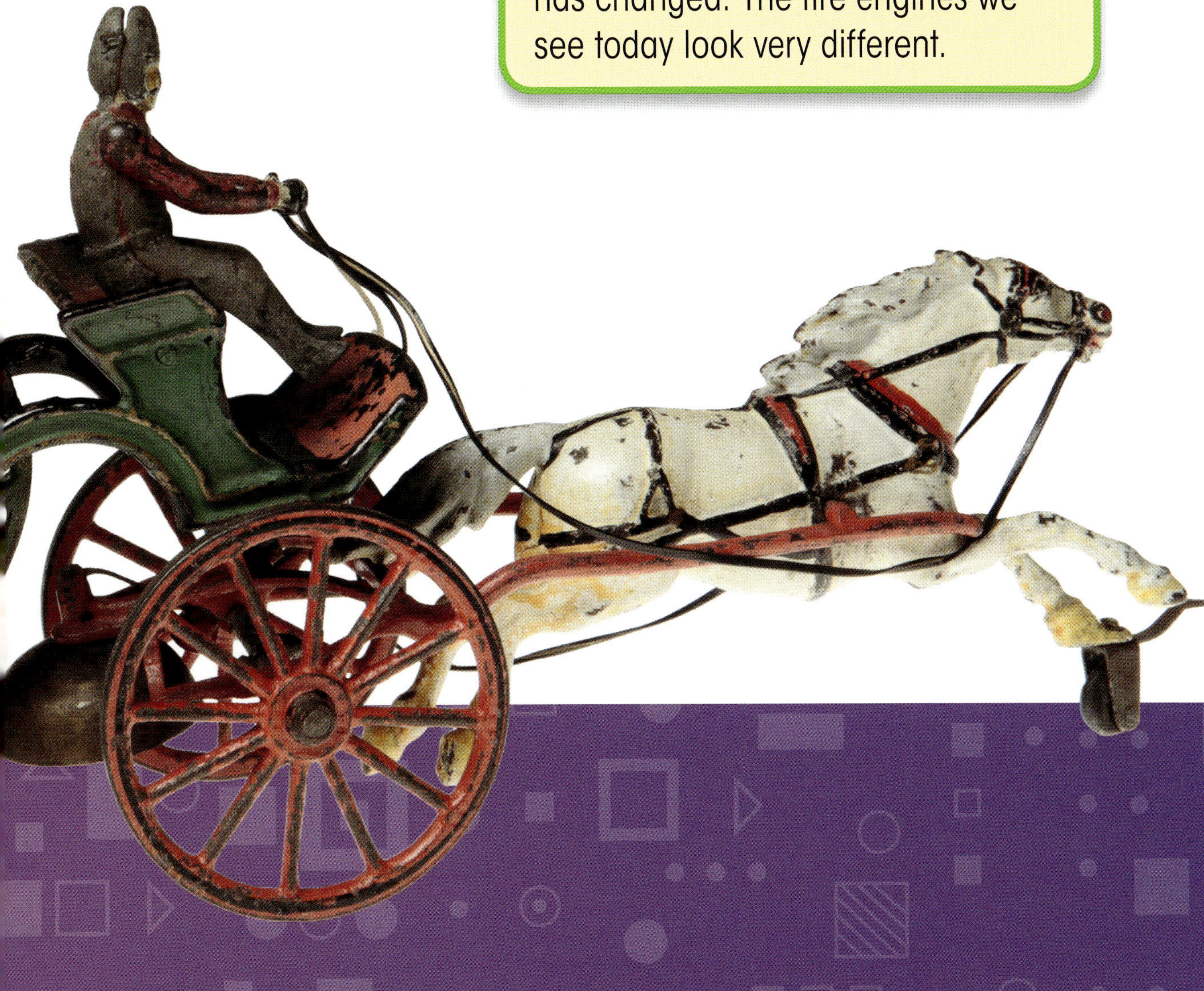

Other primary sources can help us learn more about an artifact. A catalog from 1902 is a primary source document. It has information about the cost of toys and other details about the toys from long ago. A catalog might also lead us to ask even more questions and look at more primary sources.

Pages from a 1902 Sears catalog

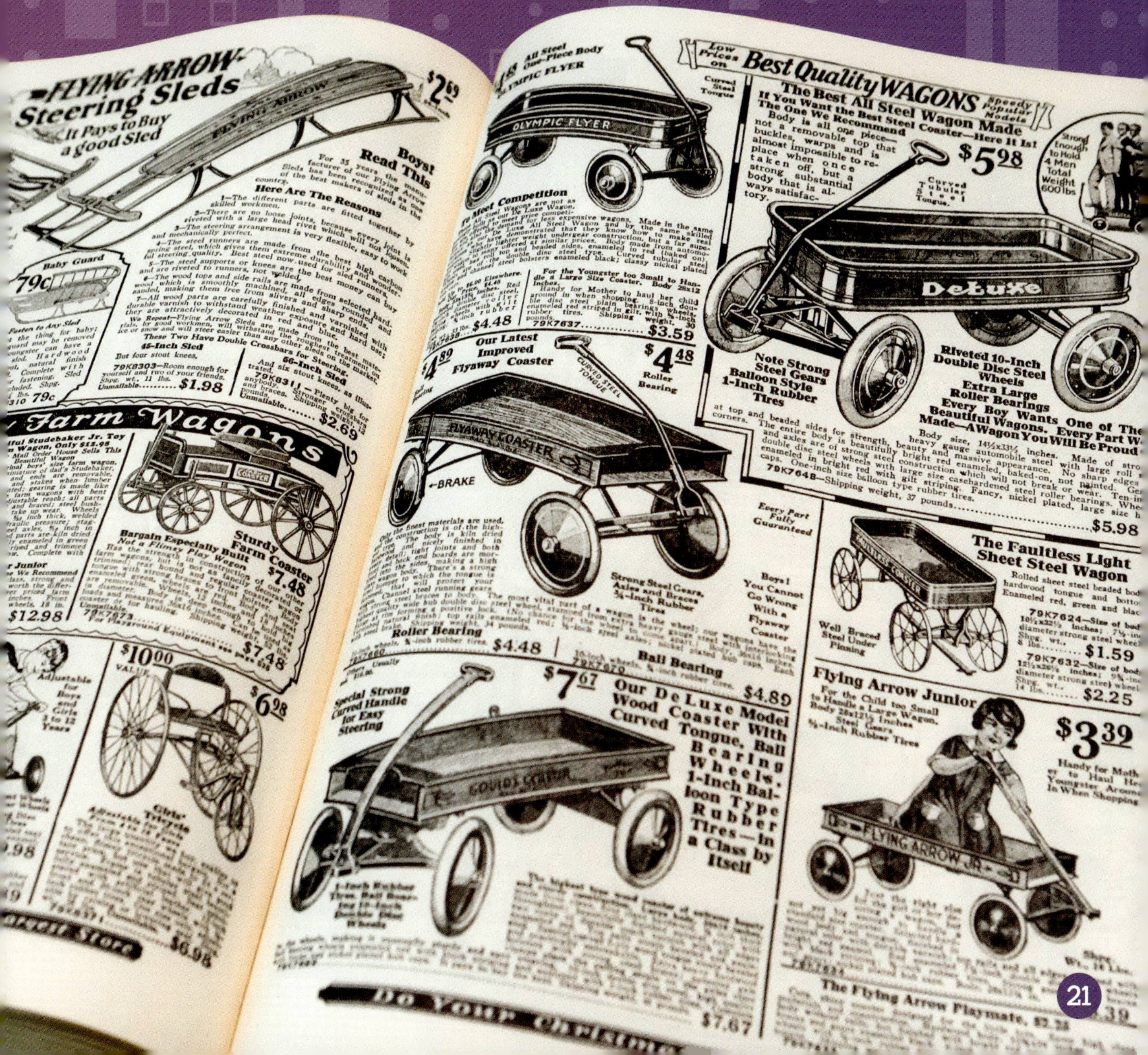

Glossary

artifact—an object that has been made or shaped by humans

Declaration of Independence—a document signed on July 4, 1776, declaring the United States' independence from British rule

examine—to inspect or look at something carefully

historian—a person who studies history and writes about it

primary source—an original, first-hand account of an event or time period

Read More

Clapper, Nikki Bruno. *Learning About Primary Sources.* Media Literacy for Kids. North Mankato, Minn.: Capstone Press, 2016.

Hurt, Avery Elizabeth. *What Are Artifacts?* Let's Find Out! New York: Britannica Educational Publishing, 2019.

Internet Sites

Use FactHound to find Internet sites related to this book.

Visit *www.facthound.com*

Just type in 9781977102904 and go.

Critical Thinking Questions

1. Where do you think would be a good place to find artifacts?
2. Future historians may study artifacts from our time period. What will these items tell them about us?
3. Which artifact shown in the book do you think gives us the most information about the past? Why?

Index